Module 2 • Set 3 • Curious Creatures

CONTENTS

This book belongs to

. . . .

Great Minds® is the creator of *Eureka Math*®, *Wit & Wisdom*®, *Alexandria Plan*™, and *PhD Science*™.

Geodes® are published by Great Minds in association with Wilson Language Training, publisher of Fundations®.

Credits

- *Small Wonders*: folio icon, Alfmaler/Shutterstock.com; pp. 6–7, 9, 11, illustrations by Beatrix Potter © Frederick Warne & Co., Courtesy F. Warne & Co. & the Victoria & Albert Museum; p. 12, illustration from *The Tale of Peter Rabbit* by Beatrix Potter © Frederick Warne & Co., 2002; More page, photo of Beatrix Potter © Frederick Warne & Co., courtesy of a private collector

- *A Wish to Fly*: p. 14 (top), Drew Horne/Shutterstock.com, (second from top), Julie A. Curtis/Shutterstock.com, (third from top), vagabond54/Shutterstock.com, (bottom), Deep Desert Photography/Shutterstock.com; More page, Mockingbird, color engraving by R. Havell, after drawing by John J. Audubon. Illus. in: The birds of America by John James Audubon. 4 vol. London, 1827-1838, (Elephant Folio), Vol. I, Pl. 21. Photo courtesy Library of Congress, Prints & Photographs Division, [LC-USZC4-855].

- *One Look*: folio icon, Volosovich Igor/Shutterstock.com; More page, David Doubilet/National Geographic/Getty Images

- *Slug Study*: More page, photo by Ezume Images/Shutterstock.com

Small Wonders

by Emily Climer   illustrated by
                          Ali Douglass

With a pen in hand,
she sits to draw.

She sits very still . . .
and looks.

1

Beatrix Potter loves
to draw animals.
And she does so
with such care.

2

In the grass,
she hunts for pets
with her brother.

The two of them have
lots of pets.

When they spot a frog,

they act fast.

They run to trap it

in a net.

What a thrill

to see it up close!

Its legs are long,

but they bend

so it can jump.

She *just must* draw it.

When she draws,
she sees as much
as she can.

In this one,
she jots a thin line
for each twig.

She also tends
to the bugs
with care.

As she grows up,
her skills grow, too.

Beatrix Potter was 9 when she drew this.

With this bat,
she observes
the small things.

It has claws that can grip.
And eyes that flash!

Its big ears are soft
with pink fuzz.

Beatrix Potter was 22 when she drew this.

She does not miss a thing.

When she draws,

Beatrix sees the small wonders—

in pigs

and hens

and cats . . .

Come dance a jig to my Grannys' Pig.

Beatrix Potter was 39 when she drew this.

Beatrix Potter was 35 when she drew this.

. . . and in rabbits.

Over time,

she comes to share

with the world

what she sees.

Kids love her animals.
When they see them,
they sit very still . . .
and look.

More

Beatrix Potter's early artwork focused on nature. As a young woman, she studied mushrooms. She painted fungi with scientific accuracy. This further developed her skill to create detailed illustrations.

Potter's life changed when she sent a letter to a friend's sick child. In the illustrated letter, she told the story of a naughty rabbit. The child loved the story, and Potter was encouraged to write more. She turned the story into her first book, *The Tale of Peter Rabbit.*

Six publishers rejected the book, so Potter used her own money to publish the tale. All 250 copies sold fast. Soon another company offered to publish it. Potter wrote and illustrated 22 more animal tales.

Más

Las primeras ilustraciones de Beatrix Potter se centraban en la naturaleza. De joven, estudió las setas. Las pintaba con la precisión de un científico. Esto la ayudó a desarrollar su talento para crear ilustraciones minuciosas.

La vida de Potter cambió cuando le envió una carta al hijo enfermo de una amiga. En esta carta ilustrada, le contaba la historia de un conejo travieso. Al niño le encantó la historia y esto motivó a Potter a seguir escribiendo. Esta historia se convirtió en su primer libro, *The Tale of Peter Rabbit* (*El cuento de Pedrito Conejo*).

Seis editoriales rechazaron el libro, por lo que Potter usó su propio dinero para publicar el cuento. Las 250 copias se vendieron rápidamente. Al poco tiempo, otra compañía le ofreció publicarlo. Potter escribió e ilustró otros 22 cuentos de animales.

A Wish to Fly

by Rachel Hylton • illustrated by Jordi Solano

I wish I had wings.

I flap and flap,

but I am stuck on this bench.

No wings for me.

Mrs. B puts a page on my desk.

It is a bird on a twig.

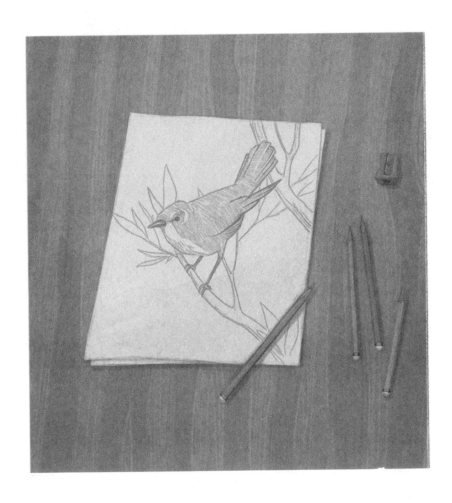

I know this bird!

I hear it sing when I am in bed.

Chat-chat-chat.

Trill-trill-trill.

3

I color the bird just like it is.

Black wings. Gray chest.

Mrs. B gives me lots of bird books.
I read and read.

I find out that I could study birds.

Ducks.

Gulls.

Chats.

It could be my job!

I could learn . . .

where to find nests,

how to make calls and songs,

and how to keep a habitat safe.

Now I am a man.

It is my job to track birds.

To observe them.

To protect them.

Chip-chip-chip!

I spot a finch in a nest.

I *pish-pish-pish* with my lips.

She flits by to check me out.

10

She has six eggs.

I jot that on my pad.

On my next walk,

I will check back for chicks.

I find a thrush.

He fluffs his chest and sings.

Pit-pit!

I spot him catch a moth.

I jot that on my pad, too.

I still wish I had wings,

but I am not stuck.

When I am with birds,

I fly.

About the Animals

mockingbird

finch

thrush

chat

More

This book is inspired by Dr. J. Drew Lanham. He teaches at Clemson University, where he is a professor of wildlife ecology. Dr. Lanham studies how changes in a forest affect the wild animals that live in it. Of all the wild animals he studies, Lanham is most interested in birds. Even as a child, he loved observing birds. The science of studying birds is called ornithology.

Ornithologists observe birds for many reasons. Some study how mockingbirds copy the sounds they hear. Mockingbirds can mimic up to 35 different birds. They can also copy the sounds of car alarms. Studying how birds learn new songs may help scientists understand how human brains make sense of new information.

Más

Este libro se inspira en el Dr. J. Drew Lanham. El Dr. Lanham da
clases en la Universidad de Clemson donde es profesor de Ecología de
la Fauna Silvestre. Estudia cómo los cambios en un bosque afectan
a los animales salvajes que en él habitan. De todos los animales que
estudia, los que más le interesan son los pájaros. Ya desde niño, le
gustaba observar los pájaros. La ciencia que estudia los pájaros se
llama ornitología.

Los ornitólogos observan los pájaros por diversos motivos. Algunos
estudian cómo los sinsontes copian los sonidos que escuchan. Los
sinsontes pueden replicar el canto de hasta 35 pájaros. También
imitan el sonido de las alarmas de los autos. Estudiar cómo los
pájaros aprenden nuevos cantos puede ayudar a los científicos a
entender cómo el cerebro humano comprende nueva información.

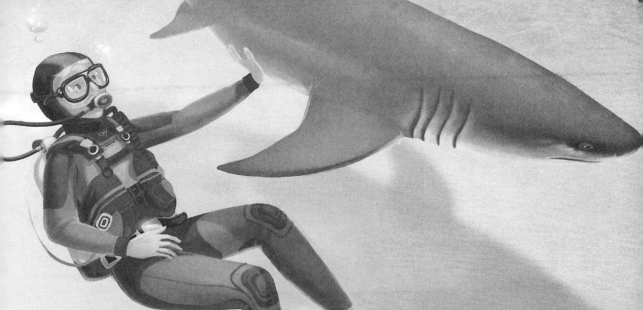

ONE LOOK

TREE LIBERATORE
JUAN M. MORENO

All it took was one look in the big tank.

She was only 9.

Sharks cast a spell on her.

1

She put her chin up to the thick glass.
To swim with them would be a thrill!

2

"One day I will," she said.

3

Eugenie Clark had a plan.

She went to college.

Not a lot of girls were there to study fish.

But she was.

Her dream was to know them—
not from a desk, but in the sea.

5

Then she got her wish.

She went on a scuba trip.

She went to the depth of the sea.

The fish swam up to her mask.

The sharks sped past her.

It was a thrill.

And, it was a real job!

She had a hunch:

There was more to a shark than its bite.

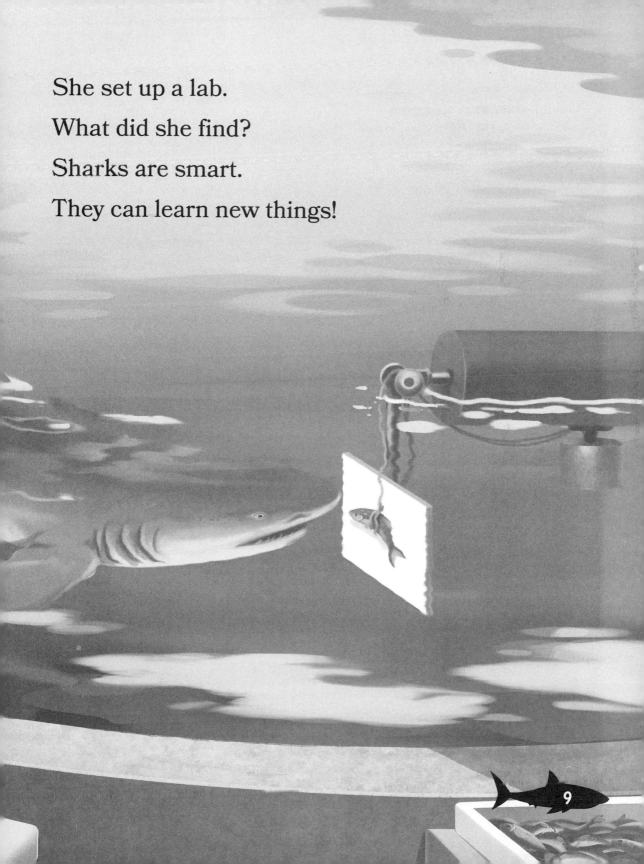

She set up a lab.

What did she find?

Sharks are smart.

They can learn new things!

9

She had respect for them.

This was new thinking.

Eugenie had a very long life.

She spent much of it in the sea.

She did more than 70 dives.
She was a whiz at that!

12

For her, sharks were the best thing of all.

She felt she had to protect them.

That was her quest.

This is why we call her the Shark Lady.

Just think—it can all begin with one look in a big tank!

MORE

Eugenie Clark always loved the sea. As a child, she had her own small aquarium. She learned to swim before she was two years old.

When Clark grew up, she earned a doctorate in zoology—the study of animals. She focused on the fish she loved as a child, including platies and swordtails. She went on to discover several species of fish. Four species are named after her.

Dr. Clark encountered a variety of sea life during her many deep-sea dives. She even rode a whale shark. This gentle shark is the largest fish in the world. It can grow to be longer than 50 feet and can weigh more than 40,000 pounds. Clark was so passionate about exploring the sea that she continued diving into her 90s. Dr. Clark credited her Japanese heritage with influencing her curiosity about the ocean.

JAPAN - MARCH 23: Dr. Eugenie Clark examines deep water sharks from Suruga Bay.

Más

Eugenie Clark siempré amó el mar. De niña, tenía su propia pecera pequeña. Aprendió a nadar antes de cumplir dos años.

Cuando Clark creció, obtuvo un doctorado en Zoología, que es la rama que estudia los los animales. Se especializó en los peces que amaba de niña, incluidos el platy y el pez cola de espada. Luego descubrió varias especies de peces. Hay cuatro especies que llevan su nombre.

La Dra. Clark encontró una gran variedad de vida marina mientras buceaba en aguas profundas. Hasta nadó sobre un tiburón ballena. Este tiburón dócil es el más grande del mundo. Puede llegar a medir más de 50 pies y pesar más de 40,000 libras. A Clark le apasionaba tanto explorar el mar que siguió buceando hasta los 90 años. La Dra. Clark atribuyó su curiosidad por el océano a la influencia de su ascendencia japonesa.

Slug Study

written by Lior Klirs

illustrations by Alex Paterson

I am Sal.

I am six,

and I love science.

My mom is a scientist.

When I am big,

I want to be like her.

2

But now,

I think I am too small

to help.

Then Mom tells me
the museum has a job for kids.
We must get slugs!

The people at the museum will observe
our slugs.

They will find facts
to help slugs
and protect their habitats.

Be a Citizen Scientist

Why?

Well, slugs can be pests.

But they also
snack on old plants.

That helps fresh ones pop up.

All animals have a job.

Now I have a job, too.

I get my log
and a pen.
I sit on a bench
in the grass.
Then I list
what I observe.

Day 1:

No slugs.

Hot.

Too much sun!

I will go in for lunch.

Day 2:

I hunt.

Where are the slugs?

Not a hint!

Not fun!

Mom says to be a scientist,
you must have grit.

Day 3:

Try again.
I sit still.
I scan a shrub.

There, a slug!
It is yellow
with black spots.

I jump—trap it in a cup.

It sheds some slime.

What a thrill!

Mom and I go
to the museum.
We hand over the slug.
They will put it
in a garden
to observe it.

I am Sal.

I am six,

and now

I am a scientist.

More

Slugs are not just slimy creatures that eat garden plants. These animals play an important role in an ecosystem, a community of living things and their environment. Slugs eat rotting plants and help enrich the soil. They are also food for birds and toads.

Scientists learn more about slugs by counting them. The slug's habitat is shrinking. When cities build new roads and buildings, they cut down the forests and trees where slugs live. Scientists study the effects of new construction by counting slugs found in different locations.

In Los Angeles, California, the public can participate in the SLIME (Snails and Slugs Living in Metropolitan Environments) project. Citizen scientist projects like this encourage people to explore nature where they live.

Más

Las babosas no son solo criaturas viscosas que se comen las plantas del jardín. Estos animales cumplen una función muy importante en un ecosistema, una comunidad de organismos vivos y sus entornos. Las babosas comen plantas en descomposición y así ayudan a enriquecer la tierra. También son el alimento de los pájaros y los sapos.

Los científicos aprenden más sobre las babosas al contarlas. Su hábitat se está reduciendo. Cuando los humanos construyen calles y edificios nuevos, talan los bosques y los árboles donde habitan las babosas. Los científicos cuentan el número de babosas en diversas zonas para determinar el impacto de las nuevas construcciones.

En Los Ángeles, California, el proyecto *Snails and Slugs Living in Metropolitan Environments* (Caracoles y Babosas en Entornos Metropolitanos, SLIME, por sus siglas en inglés) está abierto a la participación del público. Los proyectos científicos para ciudadanos, como este, motivan a la gente a explorar la naturaleza del lugar donde viven.